P9-EDG-764

Team Spirit ● College Football

The
Notre Dame®
Fighting Irish™

BY
MARK STEWART

Content Consultant
Kent Stephens
College Football Hall of Fame

NORWOOD HOUSE PRESS
CHICAGO, ILLINOIS

Norwood House Press
P.O. Box 316598
Chicago, Illinois 60631

For information regarding Norwood House Press, please visit our website at:
www.norwoodhousepress.com or call 866-565-2900.

All photos courtesy of Getty Images except the following:
Author's Collection (6, 28, 40), Classic Games (9, 37 top right),
University of Notre Dame (7, 16, 17, 22, 25, 29, 31), Associated Press (34),
Fawcett Publications, Inc. (14), Topps, Inc. (21, 23, 39, 41 bottom left),
Collegiate Collection (24, 36 right, 41 bottom right), National Chicle Co. (36 left),
Macfadden-Bartell Corp. (37 top left), The Downtown Athletic Club of New York City, Inc. (41 top right).
Cover Photo: Matthew Stockman/Getty Images

Special thanks to Topps, Inc.

Editor: Mike Kennedy
Designer: Ron Jaffe
Project Management: Black Book Partners, LLC.
Editorial Production: Jessica McCulloch
Research: Joshua Zaffos
Special thanks to R. Peter Dales

Library of Congress Cataloging-in-Publication Data

Stewart, Mark, 1960-
   The Notre Dame Fighting Irish / by Mark Stewart ; content consultant,
Kent Stephens.
       p. cm. -- (Team spirit--college football)
   Includes bibliographical references and index.
   Summary: "Presents the history and accomplishments of The University of
Notre Dame Fighting Irish football team. Includes highlights of players,
coaches, and awards, longstanding rivalries, quotes, timeline, maps,
glossary, and websites"--Provided by publisher.
   ISBN-13: 978-1-59953-279-0 (library edition : alk. paper)
   ISBN-10: 1-59953-279-4 (library edition : alk. paper)
   1. University of Notre Dame--Football--Juvenile literature. 2. Notre Dame
Fighting Irish (Football team)--Juvenile literature. I. Stephens, Kent,
1953- II. Title.
   GV958.N6S75 2010
   796.332'630977289--dc22

                                                    2010004365

Manufactured in the United States of America in North Mankato, Minnesota.
159N—072010

COVER PHOTO: The Fighting Irish celebrate a good play during a 2007 game.

Table of Contents

SPORTS WORDS & VOCABULARY WORDS: In this book, you will find many words that are new to you. You may also see familiar words used in new ways. The glossary on page 46 gives the meanings of football words, as well as "everyday" words that have special football meanings. These words appear in **bold type** throughout the book. The glossary on page 47 gives the meanings of vocabulary words that are not related to football. They appear in ***bold italic type*** throughout the book.

Meet the Fighting Irish ™

Winning comes naturally to the football team at the University of Notre Dame. It has for more than a *century*. Of course, no one likes losing. Not the players at Notre Dame. Not the students. And, most of all, not the fans. Supporters of the team live in every state in America and almost every country in the world. On game day, millions of people stop whatever they are doing to root for the Fighting Irish.

The Notre Dame *campus* is located in South Bend, Indiana. It holds a special place in football history. Many great coaches and players have worn the team's famous gold helmet. At Notre Dame, *tradition* and teamwork come together in a *unique* way.

This book tells the story of the Fighting Irish. Their players win trophies and awards. Their teams win championships. Their coaches change the game. That is why kids everywhere dream of strapping on a Notre Dame helmet and taking the field for the Fighting Irish.

During the week, Notre Dame players and fans see each other in class and on campus. On game day, they celebrate together when the team scores a touchdown.

Way Back When

Notre Dame's first football squad suited up in 1887. Back then, the school's teams were known as the Catholics. Later, they were called the Ramblers. Newspaper writers had a different idea. They nicknamed Notre Dame's players the "Fighting Irish." As the team got better, the players and fans liked the name more and more. In 1927, it became official.

By then, Knute Rockne had turned Notre Dame into the nation's top team— first as a player and then as head coach. Rockne lost only 12 games in his 13 years as the coach of the Fighting Irish. He led the school to five **undefeated** seasons and three national championships.

Rockne's best season as a coach may have been 1924. The team's stars were quarterback Harry Stuhldreher and running backs Elmer Layden, Jim Crowley, and Don Miller. The famous sportswriter Grantland Rice nicknamed them the "Four Horsemen" after a story from the Bible.

Rockne died in a plane crash in 1931, but Notre Dame football carried on. Great players during the **decades** that followed included: linemen George Connor and Bill Fischer; ends Wayne Millner, Bob Dove, and Leon Hart; running back Emil Sitko; and quarterbacks Angelo Bertelli, Bob Williams, and Johnny Lujack. From 1943 to 1949, coach Frank Leahy guided Notre Dame to the national championship four times.

The parade of stars for the Fighting Irish continued during the 1950s and early 1960s. Johnny Lattner, Paul Hornung, Nick Pietrosante, Daryle Lamonica, and Nick Buoniconti were among the best players in the country. When Ara Parseghian took over as coach in the 1960s, Notre Dame enjoyed a new **era** of success.

LEFT: This poster advertises a special train during the 1920s that brought fans from Chicago, Illinois to Notre Dame games.
ABOVE: Knute Rockne watches the "Four Horsemen" practice a play.

Parseghian built balanced teams that were strong on offense and defense. Notre Dame's stars included quarterbacks John Huarte and Terry Hanratty, running back Nick Eddy, and defensive stars Nick Rassas, Alan Page, and Jim Lynch. The Fighting Irish won their eighth national championship in 1966.

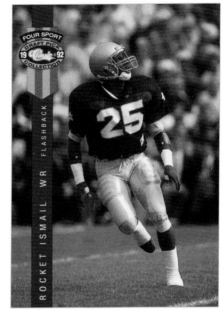

The 1970s brought two more national championships to South Bend. During the decade, Notre Dame was led by Walt Patulski, Ross Browner, Steve Niehaus, and Bob Golic on defense. The offense was guided by quarterbacks Joe Theismann, Tom Clements, and Joe Montana, and two great tight ends, Dave Casper and Ken MacAfee. In the 1980s, players such as Mark Bavaro, Bob Crable, Dave Duerson, and Allen Pinkett starred for the Fighting Irish.

Coach Lou Holtz led Notre Dame to its 11th national championship in 1988. That team's leaders were quarterback Tony Rice, running back Ricky Watters, receiver Raghib "Rocket" Ismail, and defensive stars Todd Lyght, Michael Stonebreaker, and Chris Zorich. Many more stars played for Holtz, including Rick Mirer, Jerome Bettis, Tim Brown, Andy Heck, Bryant Young, and Bobby Taylor. Each was an **All-American** for the Fighting Irish. They helped Notre Dame stay near the top of college football season after season.

LEFT: Tim Brown looks for an opening in the defense.   **ABOVE**: This trading card shows Rocket Ismail waiting to catch a punt.

21st Century

Throughout history, Notre Dame football has been known for its consistency. Year in and year out, the Fighting Irish find good players and teach them how to play winning football. As the team began its third century, however, it struggled to win. In some years, the coaches and players worked as one, and the results were fantastic. In other years, the team fell short of expectations.

The good news was that great players kept coming to Notre Dame—and fans kept filling the stadium. They cheered for exciting stars such as Jimmy Clausen, Anthony Fasano, Ryan Grant, Julius Jones, Brady Quinn, Golden Tate, Justin Tuck, Jeff Samardzija, and Anthony Weaver.

History is a good teacher. In the case of Notre Dame football, it shows that, in any given season, the Fighting Irish can put together a strong **roster** and form a championship team. That is why—for millions of fans around the country and around the world—time stands still on Saturday afternoons when Notre Dame takes the field.

Brady Quinn leads the Fighting Irish onto the field for a 2005 game in their famous green and gold uniforms.

Home Turf

For many years, Notre Dame played its home games at Cartier Field. By the 1920s, the stadium could no longer hold the large crowds that rooted for the Fighting Irish. In 1930, the team moved into Notre Dame Stadium, the same field the school uses today. Knute Rockne designed the stadium. Cartier Field became the team's practice field.

Notre Dame Stadium is one of the oldest and most beautiful stadiums in college football. Unlike stadiums at other schools, it does not have large and expensive video scoreboards. Notre Dame prefers that its stadium has an old-time feel to it. When students and fans look around the field today, it seems like they have been transported back in time.

BY THE NUMBERS

- *In 1997, Notre Dame Stadium was **renovated** and 21,720 seats were added.*
- *The stadium now has 80,795 seats for football.*
- *More than 700,000 bricks were used to enlarge the stadium.*

Fans fill Notre Dame Stadium for a 2009 game. They love the stadium's old-time feel.

Dressed for Success

Notre Dame's uniform is one of the most famous—and simplest—in college football. The team's home jersey is blue with white numbers and gold trim. The road jersey is white with blue numbers and gold trim. The players wear gold pants for all games. A small *ND* logo appears near the collar of the jersey and also on the side of the pants. On special occasions, the Fighting Irish wear green jerseys with gold numbers. The school has used these uniforms from time to time for more than 80 years.

Notre Dame's gold helmets aren't just gold colored. The paint used by team managers before each game contains real gold. The gold reminds students and players of the famous Golden Dome on campus.

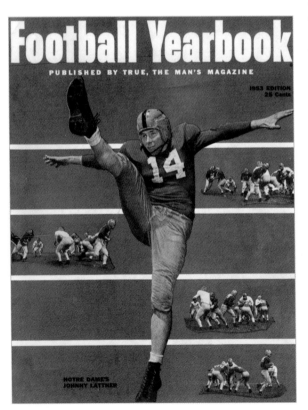

Johnny Lattner models the Notre Dame home uniform from the early 1950s.

UNIFORM BASICS

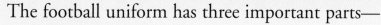

The football uniform has three important parts—

- Helmet
- Jersey
- Pants

Helmets used to be made out of leather, and they did not have facemasks—ouch! Today, helmets are made of super-strong plastic. The uniform top, or jersey, is made of thick fabric. It fits snugly around a player so that tacklers cannot grab it and pull him down. The pants come down just over the knees.

There is a lot more to a football uniform than what you see on the outside. Air can be pumped inside the helmet to give it a snug, padded fit. The jersey covers shoulder pads, and sometimes a rib protector called a flak jacket. The pants include pads that protect the hips, thighs, *tailbone*, and knees.

Football teams have two sets of uniforms— one dark and one light. This makes it easier to tell two teams apart on the field. Almost all teams wear their dark uniforms at home and their light ones on the road.

Jimmy Clausen wears the school's 2009 home uniform.

We're Number 1!

Notre Dame won its first national championship in 1924. The Fighting Irish finished their season by beating Stanford in the **Rose Bowl**, but their toughest game came against Army. The two teams met at the Polo Grounds in New York, with more than 55,000 people in the stands. Elmer Layden scored a touchdown in the first half

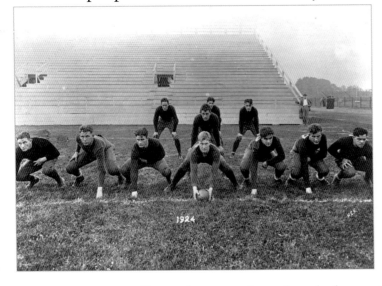

1924

to give Notre Dame a lead. In the second half, Jim Crowley ran 20 yards for another score. The Fighting Irish played great defense to secure a 13–7 win. Notre Dame fans celebrated one of the school's greatest victories ever.

In 1929, the key win in Notre Dame's second national championship season came against the University of Southern California (USC) in November. Knute Rockne had a leg infection, and his players were afraid he would not make it to the sidelines. Rockne coached the team to a thrilling 13–12 triumph

from a cot behind the bench. More than 120,000 fans packed Soldier Field in Chicago to watch the game.

In 1943, Notre Dame faced two stiff challenges on the way to the national championship. In October, the Fighting Irish rolled over Michigan, 35–12. A month later, they played Iowa Pre-Flight, a military team that included college stars and players from the **National Football League (NFL)** who joined the Navy during World War II. Notre Dame, by contrast, had just lost starting quarterback Angelo Bertelli to the military. Young Johnny Lujack stepped in and played a great game. So did running backs Creighton Miller, Julie Rykovich, and Jim Mello. Miller's touchdown late in the game gave Notre Dame a 14–13 win. The Fighting Irish ended the season at 9–1 and were voted the best team in the country.

LEFT: The 1924 champs line up on offense.   **ABOVE**: Creighton Miller dives for a touchdown against Michigan in 1943.

Go-To Guys

JOHNNY LUJACK   Quarterback

• BORN: 1/4/1925 • PLAYED FOR VARSITY: 1943 & 1946–1947

Johnny Lujack led the Fighting Irish to the national championship in each of his three seasons. He won the **Heisman Trophy** as a senior in 1947. Lujack started a tradition of great quarterbacks from western Pennsylvania. **Hall of Famers** Johnny Unitas, Joe Namath, Joe Montana, and Dan Marino followed in his footsteps.

GEORGE CONNOR   Lineman

• BORN: 1/21/1925 • DIED: 3/31/2003 • PLAYED FOR VARSITY: 1946–1947

George Connor began his college career at Holy Cross but switched to Notre Dame after serving in World War II. His great defense helped the Fighting Irish win the national championship two years in a row. Connor won the **Outland Trophy** in 1946.

LEON HART   Receiver/Defensive Lineman

• BORN: 11/2/1928 • DIED: 9/24/2002 • PLAYED FOR VARSITY: 1946–1949

Leon Hart was a great **all-around** star. He was a good blocker and receiver on offense and a great tackler on defense. Hart was a member of three championship teams at Notre Dame and won the Heisman Trophy in 1949.

JOHNNY LATTNER — Running Back/Defensive Back

• BORN: 10/24/1932 • PLAYED FOR VARSITY: 1951–1953

Johnny Lattner was a swift and powerful runner who won the Heisman Trophy in 1953. That year, he led Notre Dame to an undefeated season. Lattner was a **versatile** star who often played 60 minutes a game.

PAUL HORNUNG — Quarterback/Defensive Back

• BORN: 12/23/1935

• PLAYED FOR VARSITY: 1954–1956

Paul Hornung

In 1956, Paul Hornung was a one-man wrecking crew. He led the Fighting Irish in passing yards, rushing yards, points, kickoff returns, and punt returns. On defense, he was second in **interceptions** and tackles. Though Notre Dame went 2–8, Hornung won the Heisman Trophy.

TIM BROWN — Receiver/Kick Returner

• BORN: 7/22/1966 • PLAYED FOR VARSITY: 1984–1987

Many fans rate Tim Brown as the best receiver in the history of college football. His nickname in South Bend was "Touchdown Timmy." He set a school record with over 5,000 **all-purpose yards**. Brown won the Heisman Trophy in 1987.

WAYNE MILLNER   Receiver/Defensive Lineman

• Born: 1/31/1913   • Died: 11/19/1976   • Played for Varsity: 1933–1935

Wayne Millner could win games by catching touchdown passes or by making tackles and blocking kicks. Against Army in his first season, Millner batted down a punt and returned it for a touchdown with a minute to play. His great play gave Notre Dame a 13–12 victory.

TERRY HANRATTY   Quarterback

• Born: 1/19/1948   • Played for Varsity: 1966–1968

Terry Hanratty had a cool head and a powerful arm. He teamed up with receiver Jim Seymour to give the Fighting Irish a great passing attack.

Hanratty was the quarterback on Notre Dame's 1966 championship team.

JOE THEISMANN   Quarterback

• Born: 9/9/1949

• Played for Varsity: 1968–1970

Joe Theismann was smart and played with a big heart. Theismann set school records for passing yards and touchdowns as a senior in 1970. He led Notre Dame to a 10–1 record that year.

LEFT: Joe Theismann
RIGHT: Brady Quinn

JOE MONTANA   **Quarterback**

- BORN: 6/11/1956 • PLAYED FOR VARSITY: 1975–1978

Joe Montana was a **second-string** quarterback when the 1977 season began. By the end of the year, he was the starter, and Notre Dame was the best team in the country. Montana specialized in leading the Fighting Irish to amazing *comeback* victories.

RAGHIB "ROCKET" ISMAIL   **Receiver/Kick Returner**

- BORN: 11/18/1969 • PLAYED FOR VARSITY: 1988–1990

Rocket Ismail had the speed of an ***Olympic*** sprinter. At Notre Dame, he was the most dangerous offensive player in college football. Ismail averaged over 22 yards per catch and twice returned two kicks for touchdowns in the same game.

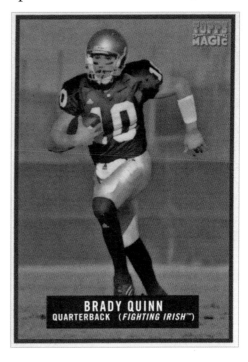

BRADY QUINN   **Quarterback**

- BORN: 10/27/1984
- PLAYED FOR VARSITY: 2003–2006

Brady Quinn could throw a touchdown pass at any time, from anywhere on the field. He broke more than 30 school records during his career. As a senior, Quinn threw for 37 touchdowns and nearly 3,500 yards.

BRADY QUINN
QUARTERBACK (*FIGHTING IRISH*™)

IMPACT PLAYERS
These Notre Dame stars loved the hard hitting of college football!

GEORGE TRAFTON   Lineman

• BORN: 12/6/1896 • DIED: 9/5/1971 • PLAYED FOR VARSITY: 1919

George Trafton was once called the "meanest, toughest player alive." And that was a teammate talking! Trafton was one of the first centers to snap the ball with one hand and one of the first defensive linemen to roam the field like a linebacker.

ELMER LAYDEN   Running Back/Defensive Back

ELMER LAYDEN

• BORN: 5/4/1903 • DIED: 6/30/1973
• PLAYED FOR VARSITY: 1922–1924

Elmer Layden was a powerful runner and an excellent defensive player. He blasted through tacklers for long gains and broke up many plays with hard tackles. In the 1925 Rose Bowl, Layden intercepted two passes and returned each for a touchdown.

JIM LYNCH   Linebacker

• BORN: 8/28/1945
• PLAYED FOR VARSITY: 1964–1966

The Fighting Irish went undefeated in 1966 thanks to their rugged defense. The captain of that squad was Jim Lynch. He led the team in tackles two years in a row and won the Maxwell Award as college football's top player as a senior.

ALAN PAGE　　　　　　　　　　　Defensive End

- BORN: 8/7/1945　• PLAYED FOR VARSITY: 1964–1966

Blocking Alan Page was almost impossible. He never gave up on a play. Page was an *agile*, lightning-fast defensive end who could attack the quarterback or chase down a runner from behind.

ROSS BROWNER　　Defensive Lineman

- BORN: 3/22/1954
- PLAYED FOR VARSITY: 1973 & 1975–1977

Few Notre Dame players can say they started for four years. Ross Browner was one of them, even though he missed a season because of an injury. He was a *dominant* defender and a great leader. The Fighting Irish lost just seven games when Browner was in the **lineup**.

ALLEN PINKETT　　　　　Running Back

- BORN: 1/25/1964
- PLAYED FOR VARSITY: 1982–1985

Allen Pinkett was a quick and clever runner who piled up yards game after game. He was the first Notre Dame rusher with three 1,000-yard seasons. Pinkett set a school record with 53 touchdowns.

LEFT: Elmer Layden　　**ABOVE**: Ross Browner

On the Sidelines

Notre Dame has had some of college football's greatest coaches. Jesse Harper turned the team into a national power. One of his best players, Knute Rockne, followed him as head coach. Rockne was a master when it came to motivating his players. Before a tough battle with Army, Rockne told his players the heartbreaking story of George Gipp. Gipp was a gifted Notre Dame player who died as a young man. Rockne ordered his team to "win one for the Gipper"—and they did!

In 1941, Frank Leahy became head coach. He had once played for Rockne. Like his old coach, Leahy knew how to get the best out of his players. In 11 seasons, he led the team to four national championships. His .864 **winning percentage** is one of the best in college football history.

Ara Parseghian also coached Notre Dame for 11 seasons. During that time, the Fighting Irish won two national championships. Dan Devine followed Parseghian and did an excellent job, too. He also won a national title. Notre Dame's 11th championship came under Lou Holtz. Like Rockne and Leahy, he was a great *motivator*. Holtz won 100 games and set a high standard for those who followed—including Bob Davie, Tyrone Willingham, Charlie Weis, and Brian Kelly.

Lou Holtz squats down to get a better look at a play during a 1989 game.

Rivals

Notre Dame's greatest **rival** is Southern California. Through the 2009 season, each school had won 11 national championships, and seven players from each college had won the Heisman Trophy. Their games have produced some of the largest television audiences in history.

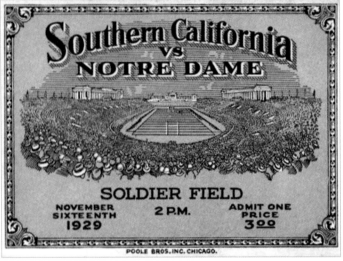

The Fighting Irish and the Trojans first played in 1926. They have met almost every year since then. The winner takes home a trophy called the Jeweled Shillelagh. From 1983 to 1993, Notre Dame won every game between the two schools. The Trojans won eight games in a row from 2002 to 2009.

Notre Dame's oldest rival is Michigan. They first squared off in 1887. In 1943, the schools met when Notre Dame was ranked first in the nation and Michigan was ranked second. The Fighting Irish won that game, and the Wolverines refused to play them again for more than 30 years. The rivalry restarted in 1978 and has been **intense**.

Among college football teams, Michigan and Notre Dame are first and second all-time in winning percentage. Every time they play, they are building on more than 120 years of success. Both schools also have very high academic standards. They always seem to be competing for the same talented student-athletes. This fuels their rivalry both on and off the field.

One of Notre Dame's most satisfying victories over the Wolverines came at Michigan in 1989. The schools were fighting for the nation's top ranking. Notre Dame won 17–10. Rocket Ismail scored both touchdowns on kickoff returns.

LEFT: A ticket from Notre Dame's game against USC in 1929.
ABOVE: Rocket Ismail is congratulated by a teammate after one of his two touchdowns against Michigan.

One Great Day

Notre Dame fans were excited when the team was invited to play against Houston in the **Cotton Bowl** after the 1978 season. One year earlier, Bob Golic and Vagas Ferguson led the Fighting Irish to an amazing 38–10 victory over Texas in the very same game to win the national championship.

The 1978 squad was not in the running for the top ranking. The Fighting Irish did have a special quarterback, however. His name was Joe Montana. The Cotton Bowl would be his final game for Notre Dame.

The Fighting Irish faced Houston on a cold and windy day. Most of the fans at the Cotton Bowl were rooting for the Cougars. Notre Dame fans were worried about Montana. He had come down with the flu and looked very weak. In the second quarter, team doctors took him to the locker room. His body temperature had dropped dangerously low.

Montana was given medical treatment at halftime. He warmed his body by drinking chicken soup. When the second half began, he was

Joe Montana looks for an open receiver during the 1979 Sugar Bowl.

still in the locker room. Meanwhile, Houston kept rolling and took a 34–12 lead.

With his team in need of a spark, Montana convinced coach Dan Devine to put him back in the game. In the fourth quarter, Notre Dame scored on a blocked punt. Montana then threw a pass to Ferguson for a two-point conversion to make the score 34–20. Next, Montana led the Fighting Irish on a 61-yard **drive**. He ran the ball into the end zone for a touchdown and threw for another two-point conversion.

Montana and the Fighting Irish got one more chance at the end of the game. With time left for one last play, he threw a touchdown pass to Kris Haines. Joe Unis kicked the extra point to give Notre Dame an incredible 35–34 victory.

It Really Happened

Notre Dame was not famous for its football teams before 1913. That year, new coach Jesse Harper scheduled a game against Army, one of the top squads in the nation. To prepare for this contest, quarterback Gus Dorais and end Knute Rockne spent the summer tossing a football back and forth on the beach. Hardly any teams used the forward pass back then. The ball was fatter than it is today, and players had a hard time throwing it accurately.

After endless hours of experimenting, Dorais found a way to loft long, spiraling passes. Rockne worked on his patterns, running to certain spots just as the ball arrived. That meant Dorais could connect with Rockne before the defense was able to react.

Notre Dame traveled to West Point, New York to play Army. The Cadets were undefeated. To them, tiny Notre Dame was a "tune-up" for later opponents. Army was bigger and stronger at every position. However, when Rockne broke free for one easy catch after another, the Cadets did not know what to do. At halftime Notre Dame led 14–13.

The Army players started the second half in a panic. Dorais continued to connect with Rockne on well-aimed throws, and Notre Dame won 35–13. In all, the quarterback completed 14 of

Knute Rockne breaks free for a long gain on a pass
against Army in 1913.

his 17 passes for 243 yards. One of these plays was a 25-yard touchdown pass to Rockne. At the time, no one could remember a longer scoring pass in a college football game.

On that day, college football changed forever. The forward pass would soon become a part of every offense. Notre Dame had made a name for itself. Everyone would remember Dorais and Rockne. And no one would ever take the Fighting Irish lightly again!

Team Spirit

After more than 12 decades of football, Notre Dame has built up a lot of team traditions. For more than 100 years, fans have been singing the "Notre Dame Victory March." It was first heard on campus in 1908.

The Notre Dame Leprechaun isn't quite that old. After using an Irish Terrier as a **mascot** for many years, the team switched to the Leprechaun in 1965. Each year dozens of students try out for the honor of being the school mascot and leading the team onto the field.

Notre Dame is a religious university. One of the oldest traditions is for the team to attend mass in the Sacred Heart Basilica before home games. Afterward, students and fans form two lines leading from the Basilica to Notre Dame Stadium. The players and coaches walk between them on their way to the field.

On their way out of the locker room for home games, players slap a sign that reads, "Play Like a Champion Today." At the end of each game, win or lose, the players turn to the student section and raise their helmets in a salute of thanks.

Notre Dame's mascot carries the school flag onto the field before a home game.

Timeline

At the end of each college season, the best teams are invited to play in special "Bowl" games, such as the Rose Bowl, **Orange Bowl**, and Sugar Bowl. Bowl games usually take place in January, but they count in the final rankings of the previous season. That means the top team in 2008 wasn't decided until early 2009. In this timeline, bowl games are listed in the year they were held.

1913
Notre Dame shocks Army with a 35–13 victory.

1941
Frank Leahy becomes head coach.

1924
Notre Dame wins its first national championship.

1930
Knute Rockne leads the team to its second national title in a row.

1943
Angelo Bertelli becomes the school's first Heisman Trophy winner.

Knute Rockne

Frank Leahy

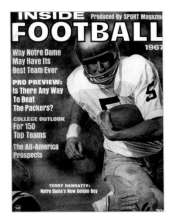

Terry Hanratty, the leader of the 1966 champs.

Jerome Bettis

1966
Notre Dame beats USC 51–0 to win the national championship.

1992
Jerome Bettis runs for three touchdowns in the Sugar Bowl.

2002
Tyrone Willingham is named Coach of the Year.

1956
Paul Hornung wins the Heisman Trophy.

1975
Dan Devine follows Ara Parseghian as head coach.

2009
Golden Tate sets a school record with 93 catches.

Golden Tate

Fun Facts

HUARTE ATTACK

In 1964, John Huarte injured his shoulder and was told by three doctors to have surgery. The quarterback ignored their advice. He led Notre Dame to nine victories in a row—and won the Heisman Trophy!

RUDY! RUDY!

As a boy, Daniel "Rudy" Ruettiger dreamed of playing football for Notre Dame. He was too small to make the squad, but he played on the scout team that helped players prepare for games. On the final home Saturday game of the 1975 season, coach Dan Devine put him in at the end of a game against Georgia Tech. With the crowd chanting, "Rudy! Rudy!," Ruettiger blew through the line and **sacked** the quarterback!

LONG TIME COMING

In 1983, Blair Kiel became the first four-year starter at quarterback since Gus Dorais in 1913.

ARMED AND DANGEROUS

Angelo Bertelli could throw the ball as well as anyone who ever played for Notre Dame. Running with the ball was another matter. Coach Frank Leahy called him the finest passer—and worst runner—he ever coached. Leahy switched to a modern **T-formation** so Bertelli could just throw the ball, and Bertelli won the Heisman Trophy!

ANGELO BERTELLI *Quarterback*

PAYBACK

In 1956, Oklahoma beat Notre Dame, 40–0. The Sooners were big favorites when they met again in 1957. The Fighting Irish shocked the football world when they won 7–0 to end Oklahoma's record 47-game winning streak.

LAW & ORDER

Creighton Miller led Notre Dame and the nation in rushing in 1943, but he decided to become a lawyer instead of joining a **professional** league. He later helped the players form the union that became the **NFL Players Association**.

LEFT: John Huarte   **ABOVE**: Angelo Bertelli

For the Record

The great Fighting Irish teams and players have left their marks on the record books. These are the "best of the best" …

NOTRE DAME AWARD WINNERS

OUTLAND TROPHY
TOP COLLEGE INTERIOR LINEMAN

George Connor	1946
Bill Fischer	1948
Ross Browner	1976

HEISMAN TROPHY
TOP COLLEGE PLAYER

Angelo Bertelli	1943
Johnny Lujack	1947
Leon Hart	1949
Johnny Lattner	1953
Paul Hornung	1956
John Huarte	1964
Tim Brown	1987

WALTER CAMP AWARD
TOP COLLEGE PLAYER

Ken MacAfee	1977
Tim Brown	1987
Rocket Ismail	1990

JOHNNY UNITAS GOLDEN ARM AWARD
TOP SENIOR QUARTERBACK

Tony Rice	1989
Brady Quinn	2006

FRED BILETNIKOFF AWARD
TOP COLLEGE RECEIVER

Golden Tate	2009

VINCE LOMBARDI AWARD
TOP COLLEGE LINEMAN OR LINEBACKER

Walt Patulski	1971
Ross Browner	1977
Chris Zorich	1990
Aaron Taylor	1993

MAXWELL AWARD
TOP COLLEGE PLAYER

Leon Hart	1949
Johnny Lattner	1952
Johnny Lattner	1953
Jim Lynch	1966
Ross Browner	1977
Brady Quinn	2006

A pennant from Notre Dame's early years.

NOTRE DAME ACHIEVEMENTS

ACHIEVEMENT	YEAR
National Champions	1924
National Champions	1929
National Champions	1930
National Champions	1943
National Champions	1946
National Champions	1947
National Champions	1949
National Champions	1966
National Champions	1973
National Champions	1977
National Champions	1988

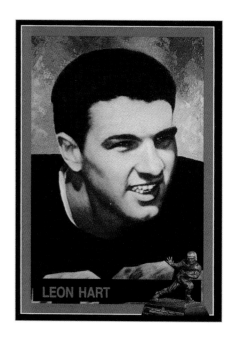

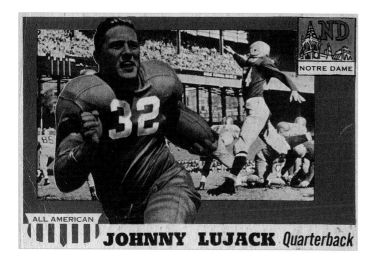

ABOVE: Johnny Lujack, the 1947 Heisman Trophy winner.
TOP RIGHT: Leon Hart, the 1949 Heisman Trophy winner.
BOTTOM RIGHT: George Connor, the 1946 Outland Trophy winner.

Top Rivals

Unlike most major universities, Notre Dame chooses not to compete in an organized football conference. The Fighting Irish have been "independent" since they began play in the 1800s. Over the years, however, the team has faced many schools regularly. In recent years, their opponents have included these fine teams …

NOTRE DAME'S TOP RIVALS

1 United States Air Force Academy Falcons
Colorado Springs, Colorado

2 United States Military Academy (Army) Black Knights
West Point, New York

3 Boston College Eagles
Chestnut Hill, Massachusetts

4 University of Michigan Wolverines
Ann Arbor, Michigan

5 Michigan State University Spartans
East Lansing, Michigan

6 United States Naval Academy (Navy) Midshipmen
Annapolis, Maryland

7 University of Pittsburgh Panthers
Pittsburgh, Pennsylvania

8 Purdue University Boilermakers
West Lafayette, Indiana

9 University of Southern California Trojans
Los Angeles, California

10 Stanford University Cardinal
Palo Alto, California

 Notre Dame Fighting Irish
South Bend, Indiana

The College Game

College football may look like the same game you see NFL teams play on Sundays, but there are some important differences. The first is that most college games take place on Saturday. This has been true for more than 100 years. Below are several other differences between college and pro football.

CLASS NOTES

College players are younger than NFL players. They are student-athletes who have graduated from high school and now play on their college's varsity team, which is the highest level of competition. Most are between the ages of 18 and 22.

College players are allowed to compete for four seasons. Each year is given a different name, or "class"—freshman (first year), sophomore (second year), junior (third year), and senior (fourth year). Players who are unable to play for the varsity can remain in the same class for an extra year. This is called "red-shirting." These players are still students and must attend classes during their extra year.

RULE BOOK

There are several differences between the rules in college football and the NFL. Here are the important ones: 1) In college, a play ends as soon as the ball carrier's knee touches the ground, even if he slips or dives. In the NFL, a player must be tackled. 2) In college, a player catching the ball near the sideline must have one foot in bounds for the reception to count. In the NFL, a player must have both feet in bounds. 3) Since 1996, tie games in college have been decided by a special overtime period. Each team is given a chance to score from its opponent's 25-yard line. In the NFL, the first team to score in overtime is the winner.

WHO'S NUMBER 1?

How is the national champion of college football decided? Each week during the season, teams are ranked from best to worst in several different polls of coaches and sportswriters. These rankings are based on many factors, including a team's record and the level of competition that it has played. At the end of the year, the two top-ranked teams play each other. The winner is declared the national champion. This tradition started in 1998 when college football began using the **Bowl Championship Series (BCS)**. Prior to that year, the top two teams did not always face each other. Sometimes, that made it very difficult to decide which school was the best.

CONFERENCE CALL

Most colleges are members of athletic conferences. Each conference represents a different part of the country. For example, the Atlantic Coast Conference is made up of teams from up and down the East Coast. Teams that belong to a conference are required to play a certain number of games against the other teams in their conference. At the end of the year, the team with the best record is crowned conference champion (unless the league holds a championship game). Teams also play schools from outside their conference. Wins and losses in those games do not count in the conference standings. However, they are very important to a team's national ranking.

BOWL GAMES

Bowl games—such as the Rose Bowl, Sugar Bowl, and Orange Bowl—are extra games played at the end of each season. Bowl games give fans a chance to see the best teams from around the country play one another. These games are scheduled during the Christmas and New Year's holiday season, so students are free to travel to the cities where bowl games are played. There are now more than 25 bowl games.

Since 1998, the BCS has selected the nation's very best teams and carefully matched them in a handful of bowl games. The BCS chooses the champions of major conferences, as well as other schools with talented teams. The two top-ranked teams meet in the BCS title game for the national championship.

Glossary

FOOTBALL WORDS TO KNOW

ALL-AMERICAN—A college player voted as the best at his position.

ALL-AROUND—Good at many different parts of the game.

ALL-PURPOSE YARDS—A statistic that measures the total yardage gained by a player.

BOWL CHAMPIONSHIP SERIES (BCS)—The system used by college football to select the best two teams to play for the national championship each season. Before the BCS came along, the national championship was unofficial, and more than one team often claimed they were the best.

COTTON BOWL—The annual bowl game played in Dallas, Texas. The first Cotton Bowl was played in 1937.

DRIVE—A series of plays by the offense that "drive" the defense back toward its own goal line.

EXTRA POINT—A kick worth one point, attempted after a touchdown.

FIELD GOAL—A goal from the field, kicked over the crossbar and between the goal posts. A field goal is worth three points.

HALL OF FAMERS—Players who have been honored as being among the greatest ever and have been voted into the Pro Football Hall of Fame.

HEISMAN TROPHY—The award given each year to the best player in college football.

INTERCEPTIONS—Passes that are caught by the defensive team.

LINEUP—The list of players in a game.

NATIONAL FOOTBALL LEAGUE (NFL)—The league that started in 1920 and is still operating today.

NFL PLAYERS ASSOCIATION—The organization that represents the NFL players in all business matters.

ORANGE BOWL—The annual bowl game played in Miami, Florida. The first Orange Bowl was played in 1935.

OUTLAND TROPHY—The award given each year to the best lineman in college football.

PROFESSIONAL—A player or team that plays a sport for money. College players are not paid, so they are considered amateurs.

ROSE BOWL—The annual bowl game played in Pasadena, California. The Tournament of Roses Parade takes place before the game. The first Rose Bowl was played in 1902.

ROSTER—The list of a team's active players.

SACKED—Tackled the quarterback behind the line of scrimmage.

SECOND-STRING—Back-up or non-starter.

SUGAR BOWL—The annual bowl game played in New Orleans, Louisiana. The first Sugar Bowl was played in 1935.

T-FORMATION—An offensive set in which three running backs line up in a row behind the quarterback to form a "T."

TWO-POINT CONVERSION—A play following a touchdown where the offense tries to cross the goal line with the ball from the 2 yard line, instead of kicking an extra point.

WINNING PERCENTAGE—A statistic that measures the number of games won by a team. A winning percentage above .500 is considered good.

OTHER WORDS TO KNOW

AGILE—Quick and graceful.

CAMPUS—The grounds and buildings of a college.

CENTURY—A period of 100 years.

COMEBACK—The process of catching up from behind.

DECADES—Periods of 10 years; also specific periods, such as the 1950s.

DOMINANT—Ruling or controlling.

ERA—A period of time in history.

INTENSE—Strong or deeply felt.

MASCOT—An animal or person believed to bring a group good luck.

MOTIVATOR—A person who inspires others to action.

OLYMPIC—Among the best in the world.

RENOVATED—Fixed and made more modern.

RIVAL—Extremely emotional competitor.

TAILBONE—The bone that protects the base of the spine.

TRADITION—A belief or custom that is handed down from generation to generation.

UNDEFEATED—Without a loss.

UNIQUE—Special or one of a kind.

VERSATILE—Able to do many things well.

Places to Go

ON THE ROAD

NOTRE DAME FIGHTING IRISH
Edison Road & Juniper Road
South Bend, Indiana 46600
(574) 631-6107

COLLEGE FOOTBALL HALL OF FAME
111 South St. Joseph Street
South Bend, Indiana 46601
(800) 440-3263

ON THE WEB

THE NOTRE DAME FIGHTING IRISH
  • *Learn more about the Fighting Irish*

www.und.com/sports/m-footbl

COLLEGE FOOTBALL HALL OF FAME
  • *Learn more about college football*

www.collegefootball.org

ON THE BOOKSHELF

To learn more about the sport of football, look for these books at your library or bookstore:

  • DeCock, Luke. *Great Teams in College Football History*. Chicago, Illinois: Raintree, 2006.
  • Yuen, Kevin. *The 10 Most Intense College Football Rivalries*. New York, New York: Franklin Watts, 2008.

Index

PAGE NUMBERS IN **BOLD** REFER TO ILLUSTRATIONS.

The Team

MARK STEWART has written more than 30 books on football players and teams, and over 100 sports books for kids. He has also interviewed dozens of athletes, politicians, and celebrities. Mark has met many of the

players in this book, including Paul Hornung, Joe Montana, Tim Brown, Ricky Watters and Rocket Ismail. In 1995, he and Fighting Irish All-American Chris Zorich co-authored a children's book about Zorich's childhood in Chicago and his years at Notre Dame. Mark comes from a family of writers. His grandfather was Sunday Editor of *The New York Time*s and his mother was Articles Editor for *Ladies' Home Journal* and *McCall's*. Mark became interested in sports during lazy summer days spent at the Connecticut home of his father's godfather, sportswriter John R. Tunis. Mark is a graduate of Duke University, with a degree in History. He lives with his wife Sarah, and daughters Mariah and Rachel, overlooking Sandy Hook, New Jersey.

One might say that KENT STEPHENS was destined to have an interest in college football. His mother chose his name while watching the 1953 Rose Bowl, in which Kent Peters was playing for the

Wisconsin Badgers. Keeping in a family tradition, Kent's niece was named for a Rose Bowl Queen when his sister was searching for a name for her baby born on New Year's Day. Kent is a graduate of both The University of Cincinnati and The Ohio State University, and is an avid fan of both the Bearcats and Buckeyes. He has been the Historian and Curator of the College Football Hall of Fame since 1990. He lives in Elkhart, Indiana with his wife Valerie.